Dinosaurs

Triceratops

Daniel Nunn

Heinemann Library
Chicago, Illinois

© 2007 Heinemann Library
a division of Reed Elsevier Inc.
Chicago, Illinois

Customer Service 888-454-2279
Visit our website at www.heinemannraintree.com

Designed by Joanna Hinton-Malivoire
Printed and bound in China by South China Printing Co. Ltd.

11 10 09 08 07
10 9 8 7 6 5 4 3 2 1

The Library of Congress has cataloged the first edition of this book as follows:
Nunn, Daniel.
  Triceratops / Daniel Nunn.
    p. cm. -- (Dinosaurs)
  Includes bibliographical references and index.
  ISBN-13: 978-1-4034-9445-0 (library binding - hardcover)
  ISBN-13: 978-1-4034-9452-8 (pbk.)
  1. Triceratops--Juvenile literature. I. Title.
  QE862.O65.N86 2007
  567.915′8--dc22
                              2006030059

Acknowledgements
The publishers would like to thank the following for permission to reproduce photographs: Alamy pp. 6, and 23 (Christian Darkin), 14 (Jeff Morgan), 19 (Phototake Inc.), 20 (JupiterMedia); Corbis pp. 7 (Gary W. Carter), 18 and 23 (Annie Griffiths Belt), 21 (Paul A. Souders), 22 (Louie Psihoyos), 22 (Philip Gould); Science Photo Library p. 12 (Christian Darkin).

Cover photograph of Triceratops reproduced with permission of Alamy/Christian Darkin.

Every effort has been made to contact copyright holders of any material reproduced in this book. Any omissions will be rectified in subsequent printings if notice is given to the publishers.

Contents

The Dinosaurs

Dinosaurs were reptiles.

Dinosaurs lived long ago.

Triceratops was a dinosaur.
Triceratops lived long ago.

Today there are no *Triceratops*.

Triceratops

Protoceratops

Some dinosaurs were small.

But *Triceratops* was big.

Triceratops had thick legs.

Triceratops lived together.

Triceratops walked slowly most of the time.

But *Triceratops* could run
fast, too.

horn

Triceratops had three horns.

Triceratops used its horns to fight other dinosaurs.

But *Triceratops* did not eat
other dinosaurs.

Triceratops ate bushes and plants.

How Do We Know?

Scientists have found fossils of *Triceratops*.

Fossils are parts of animals that lived long ago.

fossil

Fossils are in rocks.

Fossils tell us what *Triceratops* was like.

Fossil Quiz

A

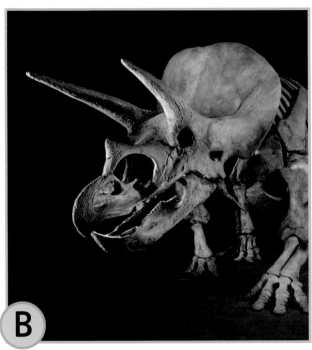

B

One of these fossils was *Triceratops*. Can you tell which one? Turn to page 24 to find out the answer.

Picture Glossary

 **dinosaur** an animal that lived long ago

 **fossil** parts of a dead animal that lived long ago

 **horn** a hard, pointed growth on an animal. Horns help protect animals.

 **reptile** animal that is cold-blooded. Snakes, lizards, turtles, and alligators are reptiles.

Index

Answer to question on page 22
Fossil B was *Triceratops*.
Fossil A was *Tyrannosaurus rex*.

Notes to Parents and Teachers

This series gives a first introduction to dinosaurs. In simple language, each book explains the physical characteristics of different dinosaurs, their behavior, and how fossils have provided a key into our knowledge of dinosaurs' existence and extinction. An expert was consulted to provide both interesting and accurate content. The text has been carefully chosen with the advice of a literacy expert to ensure that beginners can read the text independently or with moderate support.

You can support children's nonfiction literacy skills by helping students use the table of contents, picture glossary, and index.